New Year's Eve

Happy New Year

T0005228

It is New Year's Eve.

We are having a party.

3

My friends are

at the party.

We are having fun at the party.

We are playing games
at the party.

We are dancing

at the party.

We are playing
with sparklers
at the party.

Look!

It is nearly 12 o'clock.

10, 9, 8, 7, 6, 5, 4, 3, 2, 1 -

Happy New Year!